Existence And Imperfection

Jesse R Bodley

Contents

Meaning

Some will say it's bleak, reciprocal.
Everything is rocking; space is too
receding—into me.

Not a world but a word, identical—the
mystics, a few have spoken. They told
their esoteric stories just for me.

The All-Seeing Eye

So, if you ever saw me—say you never met me.
Could you recognize me? Would you remember
me as a stranger you just met, not even a block
away, just around the corner?

Should you discern, should you distinguish,
the captain of industry from the filthy panhandler,
the Master of Commerce from the thieving vagrant.
You may as well then see me, somewhere between
thine and thee, and carry on as bird and bee—as
sugar in tea, as salt in sea—as multiformity, has
homogenized at the center of you and me.

There, all eyes will see, together all as one—what
one mind wants to be when reading but only excerpts
from the testimony of Wendigo—from the gospel
of the doppelganger.

The Lemur

As it would seem
—I'm but a dreamer,
a wish upon a star,
a stone skipped
across a river.

Hanging from a tall
tree branch, just waiting
'round with eyes of glimmer,
for just one lonely centipede
to go inching near, inspiring

such coveted splendor, suggesting
not escape, but surrender, from
the untamed jungle to the seldom
rippled pond—seems, I'm a dreamer,
much like the Lemur.

Many2 Mirrors

We share this path; you and I don't always see eye to eye,
but we both agree, and I'm sure we're not mistaken, that
what little lies within our field of vision—not entirely
out of sight, nor too far above our own human cognizance,
keeps no true mystery and neither does the unseen,
and the unseen is kept hidden from those
who are not looking from the (right angle).

The line of sight has intervened; some force of questionable
good has prohibited view, from even the most watchful and
careful observer. The image is unclean and seems to have
been altered, by what or by whom remains to be (unseen) as
well, and beyond that is only a slightly imperfect surface.

Across from this doubt—some unknown distance,
there is another object which tells the same lie,
and from this askew reference point and view, we
go on forever—looking away in the other direction.

Funeral Rite

I feel trapped in this life. What rite has given in?
Those lost have always been—pacing the ledge,

always staring out and over, from this high tower.
No thoughts to calm what shouldn't have ever

become constant, no secret solemnity to never
question solace. No sacred ignominy.

What cause have I affected; what effect have I
caused? So, kill me, and let me leave.

I can see a pattern, so routine and superficial.
I can feel a dampening; I feel nothing.

The breadth of understanding is on our breath.
We love and honor every—single time of day.

There's nothing in the ending we can't catch up with.
There's no one true beginning we have ever known.

Cowards and Rogues

"Reach for doubt," cries the seeker,
crashing through the yellow door.
He's getting out—he's putting out.
(No more lights upstairs or down)
His house is warped—he is poor.
His son is dead or never born.
He knows no better nor worse;
he dreams in and out of oblivion
and knows all too well of the matter.
Burn it down. He finds out,
like fire—we all go up and down.
We're going down, all peace out.
Some go up and all come down.
"Let's go 'round," he speaks out.
Much to be learned of existence,
in as much as laying it down.

Monkey in the Middle

I played at tug of war
—drawn across the line,
as either side suggested
ever so much more.

And with such reluctance
there was so much resistance,
and for all the persistence,
I could not frame an instance.
I could not settle score,

for instance—I still drag the floor.
A center weight that cannot balance,
must it slide to either/or?
Can it maintain constant struggle?
Should it not just top the scale,
or continue on, as—go to war?

Crosswalk

The core is rotten
and the seeds have fallen
to the pavement.
Nothing grows here
but footsteps,
and occasionally the rain
will wash away their
invisible tracks.
The passersby will marvel
at one another for a moment,
and then they, too, will pass
away into obscurity.

A Gift

No more shadow, no more light—no more shade
in which to park, only silhouette, only dark.

Another figure of different height and noiseless clatter
—no remark. Oh, a fever now a lark.

Neither see nor do we hear, though so far or very near.
Either cloudy or else clear, be it thought or not less fear.

Whether be us followed or us be led, through a tunnel
or into bed. Wither flowers underfed,

whither yellow or whither red. Or better they instead,
between wakefulness and dream, still lie upon reality,

as both the sky and eyelid close with equal heaviness,
as the earth below the heavens

grows weary of starlight and shifts then to her belly, so
that starlight casts a shadow beside her twilight silhouette?

The Moment

A door slams through a draft;
an old man calls to a lost dog.
The window sings through
dancing curtains; the wind
laughs and applauds.
Pretension grabs all strings,
pulls on falling blinds.
The house is overtaken
by shutters sun bleached
and not real.

Yea

Lo and behold—the days I have sold,
neither for wealth and prosperity,
nor a poor damn fools charity,
but for all in good kind
has made up one's mind;
for one who's not wept from
the visions they've dreamt,
when—though, still of good mind,
they darkly went blind.

Existential Buddhist

I am going to walk the earth until I find something
worth not giving up, or chewing its own fingernails
off in an empty bathtub while the drain sucks
the eyeballs out of its head.

I am going to allow myself to have three small bites
of food everyday; I'm going to become an ascetic
and meditate, until I learn to control my breathing
and lower my heart rate.

I am towing a fine line and it's between two possible
extremes: one is finite and can only be aware of its
own temporary existence; the other is starlight,
which has always been faint but constant.

I will give up all earthly possessions and keep only
the clothes on my back, and the shoes on my feet
so I can walk comfortably. I may carry a backpack
to keep just a few basic supplies.

I will forsake all earthly pleasures so that I may feel
empty, every now and then, and not have to toil on
with suffering. And over time, the feelings will subside
more often, until eventually—

I won't be born at all, and won't have to die a billion times,
in between each bad decision and brutal action, and finally,
I will stop wanting to move—and not exist at all.

Zyklon B

We are all actors playing the roles,
written for obsequious children,
by the hands of playwrights,
absconded from pharaohs,
dressed in body paint.

Spouting our lines in gasps and curses,
through the height of grass—
our pretending bodies on their sides,
snickering sojourn—oh, but peeking,
like ants travel the yard by hose.

Characters quailing so upright but fair,
when bowing and scraping the earth,
a matted plaything impressed or scarred.
Our kingdom of slip and slides, and soap
—bubbles require guns and grenades.

It's water and dirt, and blue skies—all
summer long the spigots are on,
dispersing us showers—a caress of sun.
The promise of towels never to come,
always imagining our kind is good.

Salamander

The creature surfaced from still water, emerging
from the foul bottom darkness of a murky
subterranean cavern.

It detects movement afloat, disturbing the delicate,
calm nature of its existence, thus far conceived.

A protective film spreads across its eyes as it clamps its
teeth with precision on a local point of bodily distortion.

Sustained, its instinct never perceived in vain,
its reason unafflicted by purpose.
Yet, discovers a powerful current and swims along
with impunity through tunnels of monumental precedence,
engraved by ancient and forlorn prejudice.

An awareness opens up and evolves into an ever-widening
sea full of life endowed with posthumous eyes,

and it too longs to poke its head above water and discover,
yet another possible current through the terrestrial world.

It stands erect and looks upward to see the celestial heavens
above, and only dreams of what's to come.

Hairbrained Ideas

This thing in the brain,
(a spider-webbed mind
—lair of the insane.)
Figments and creatures,
and implements of torture.
It came through the window;
it creepeth past.
A recluse regresses fast.
It feeds and it waits.
It grows fat here;
it has become pregnant.

To Me

I had something but lost it
and couldn't get it back.
There's nowhere to go.
There's nothing to do
to make this better
and there's nowhere to go.
All my life I've felt I'm being
punished. Synchronicity torments
me—constant.
Now I know
that while I care,
the universe does not.
Each little bee sees by its
lonesome; every tiny ant
looks alone.

Time's Kingdom

Samurai days, battling honor—sword
displays—oh, and conquered suicide.
Lords or misfits, stone walls—keeps
with rows of figurines in lamellar armor,
always on the ready and alert for war.
Demons, wearing masks. Kabuto
helmets—attracting, deflecting attacks.
Chrysanthemums as tea or poison.
The insects buzz their brutality in falling
clouds and swarms, reflected—in water.
Entire days, tired—always entire.

A Little More Like Buddha

It's a shame and it's lame, and goddamn this thing.
Whoever thought you'd see eternity so very clearly?
You're tripping down a beach in another world, free.
You see old Sid sitting there in a trance, enlighten
—Ed Gein would have found Jesus, had he just seen
the multiplicity of our impermanence, and so sing
and dance with all dead or dying mothers at night,
like a madman ghost face in the light of the moon.
You walk right up and sit right down there beside.
The setting sun draws a brilliant line—crossing sea,
(and the magnificent shimmering of gone and can be.)
You close your eyes and never leaving, now return.
He speaks through a breeze—he says, "We've become
awakened." And you say, "Yes, but it's only in time."
He says, "Come on back now, you hear?" Just like it
were said by a 20th-century old-timer grandfather,
spanning time in a rocker—chewing tobacco spitter.
And you'd cry but it would only smear the canvas
of still and silent thoughts of the purest intentions.

Zen Moment

This is not something happening to me.
This is something that is happening.
I too am happening but not to you.
We happen to be the same thing
happening. This is happening;
this is happening. Okay.

There

You, silent mirror—cold break across
your surface, reflecting white—casting
blue seems to be the norm of things.
In your perceptual view, all the same.
You see the reverse side of picturesque.
Statues have shattered against
your truth—oh, what pieces—rubble
dinging the edges of your marvel
and beautiful despair.

Fallacy

A human is only a must,
and one replaces one.
They'll all believe at once,
a hush and those who trust
—an age of rags to dust,
the place that offal brushed.
What many seemed to one
to happen all at once.

Native Land

Come on down, now—get off of it.
That mound, who stands atop it?
Has bedlam chased a prophet up a tree?
Disguised, so don't say you saw me.
The mantid was here before we—you,
and your evil, shamanic effigy.
Destiny locks; infamy rocks—see?
This one still walks; he never talks—he,
his soliloquy.

A Scream

In a dream, floating on back,
where the stars squint through pine
—trees that always sway the wind. They
touch everything, each other—embracing
in the earth's night, rejoicing some loss
and welcoming heaven—shivering.
A silver glow before the golden light
has fallen into eyelash ladders.
To wake up sides—down, into a ride,
and we could come too. Oh, yes. We
could slide; we could all just take a ride.
And all it would take from us—our
once more, one more, (no more inside)
would be to hush and close our eyes.

Those Days

Cowards, rogues, scoundrels after dark.
Drunkards passed out, asleep in the day.
Not lain down until morning comes,
blasting degenerates in the face,
reminding them of an ambition they
once possessed but traded for nickels
and dimes bounced off of cheap whiskey
bottle caps discovered in odd places.
Pivotal times shaken off and left to roll
from the backs of broken spirits, to crash
the floor with the sounds of judgment
and disappointment. Sometimes I
miss those days.

The Kudzu and Pine Dinosaur

Take cover little brother, remember—we burned our toys and buried them as boys. We dug them up later, remember —their desecrated graves left a crater, like the asteroid that killed the dinosaurs. Grew up slamming our heads in doors like child-hood lores. Chores and bores at our cores, like memories, and so many empty church pews galore.

We wanted to believe a lack of presence would eventually leave the essence of meaning in adolescent lessons. We crashed the dirtbike and got back up, laughing at our own mortality, with beers chasing tears through mirrors, inspiring the loss of morality—we murdered false reality.

Mom and dad were lost, a fifty-fifty flattened coin toss, each and every time on tails, we learned the toll—the transparent reading of our tells. DJ was a ghost, his isolation haunted us the most. We tipped our inherited bourbon glasses and made a toast, "Damn the world!" And the masses would wither dead inside of their host. Only a few fossils would derive from most.

We passed Dad's dinosaur tree like the extinct. The missing link could not be reached—out of synchrony with life in death —we had to be free. We always sought, though we never did see. We skipped school and stayed out late; we laughed all the time, mocking fate. Driving around town in the Galaxy, just shooting stars—a wish without destiny. Our fallacy, a dream with no money.

We drank and smoked the pain away when Papah passed
away. We laughed at his funeral, (which was more like
the family tribunal.) We traded our tears for laughter and
many rotten years thereafter. We found out fast, still always
after, we lost the things which we were after. But the thing
that I remember most—and this one thing deserves a toast.
Cheers! Here's to you—little brother, and to years hereafter
of morbid laughter.

Place Setting

Old life—you beggar, you prince
of sadness; you are uselessness.
Shame, and guilty confessor to the aether.
What has become of our descendants,
and what has crystallized?
The moon was on the table, the earth
was underneath—the chandelier
was burning like the sun, and why we
became the light switch,
and what if it's too late?
Oh, all gods are sitting, or pulling up
their chairs and we're still turning over,
what's just lying there in pieces—a board
to catch our hurled same-sided dice.
But of that anomaly and other heresies,
we'll get into later, but for now, are off
the table, even though they're scattered
—all over the place.

Hidden Selections

In youth, many wander,
wrapped with a ribbon bow.
This gift presented under
the table set so low.
Tho' many quick to blunder
are forever in a row.
Yet few who cease to wonder
ever truly know.

Episodes and Epochs

His days are numbered, but this day is gone;
he lays his body down and gears his mind
for elation, as his spirit, too, becomes intoxicated.
Unaware of all but death and he is calm;
he does not fret the inevitable darkness.
He still remembers but wants to forget,
and knows that he will, and so,
he prepares himself for anything.
Old worlds, empires fallen to decadence,
burnt to cinders, and in their ruin,
new days will dawn.

A Priest Gone to Prison

I sat in a perceived, symmetrical circle,
one of the very few of his lost disciples.
We focus our minds to only breathing
as the unordained buddhist priest suggests,
and we become silence. Our duality ceases
hold of causality, (so our legs really hurt.)

Feintly, I hear a baby crying, while a cattle car
thunders by. I should not be wondering so far
in time; we should all be still without the mind.
Alright, come back, continue breathing, but
don't become distracted by why we die. No,
get a grip man, just breathe. Nothing is wrong,
only wrong attitudes.

See things differently and you will see—wait,
close your eyes, getting too caught up in other
lives. The past is right beside you, the future
still cries, even though it's in a bloody bundle.
The priest claps his hands and bows before and
soon, thereafter. We always discussed our lessons
and we often banished our visions.

He asked each of us to expound on ourselves as they
pertain to our own consciousness: one said happy;
another said blessed; still another said empty, while
the other confessed—sane? The training was rigorous
and boring; so few have experienced that stamina, that
waste. Ah, yes—well, anyway. It's all in a way its own
desire, but that is not to say we should turn undead, or
immolate what's already on fire.

Later, he asked me, "Why do you stay when I encourage
you to leave?" I answered, "I stay in spite of you." And
he said, "good." The dojo practices Kata/Form, while
the priest instructs his pupils in the way of warnings
and omens and our own nature. Our cadence became
in tune with being, as we were meant to become a spectrum.

I see him accidentally backstep onto a grasshopper, and hear
him laugh as he realizes and expresses it so. He speaks through
strangled tears, he says, " I don't know—who has worse karma,
me or him." We heard the exoskeletal body of a living, seeking
creature, crushed beneath the weight of an unholy man, guilty
of not knowing—this, the sin of all Man.

I watched the dying insect writhe its last moment as it meekly
prayed beside its own insides. We bowed in together, but we
each bowed out alone that day. That was the last time I ever
saw him in person—but I'm reminded of him often as I relive
the past and dread reincarnation.

Greys

Aye, that's another thing. For real, or believe?
What could happen—to these hatreds, and these
monstrous rejections? One for me—a liar? Yeah,
we're so connected and seen by those, whoever
may be watching. But who could hear whatever
is not spoken aloud, for fear—of others? Oh, but
whoever could deny or betray truth as evidenced
by ages of destiny, or tears from such a good
performance as ours? And yea, though we talk
our way through the valley of the shadow of doubt,
we shall fear no true objective views, but revel in our
own opinions. Neh, such things cannot exist, no way.
Too far is the earth from the heavens; no further limbs
extend past our highest tree branch—no they. Ha!
The monkey tree is the highest, a priori, and must,
of course, be shaken from time to time, and the falling
leaves account—for all we can see, only phantom—
only shadow.

A Priori

In all my wisdom, I've come to a most logical
understanding, that my monkey tree is thus
the highest, precisely because it is my own—
and, furthermore, I've concluded that because
despite all my long winded efforts to poke
the nearest star to my own with my stick,
whilst balanced precociously from my tallest
branch, that no other has achieved—what I've
hoped to do; and so I continue to ridicule
and laugh at those funny anomalies, flitting
in and out of my conscious/unconscious view,
and occupy myself with cupping my good ear
with the palm of my paw and listening in the
direction of one star at a time; and all the while,
feeling like such a clever little monkey.

Legend

Cast yourself into a lone consternation and loll
the passing away of will into isolated phantasms,
and understand my words.

Warning

This is not the place for you;
this is a solemn place, a
dreadful place. I am not
the cure for you.

This is a precursor, a hollow,
incandescent dream. These
are not your home walls, not
the rooms to better days.

Space View

We're looking at ourselves in the
mirror, and we are monsters who
wonder if they're the only ones.
We succumb to death, regardless
of how afraid we are of peace.
We seclude ourselves in freezing
isolation, and then dare ourselves
not to go too deep—and then
we fall asleep.

In a Past Life

First, we smoked weed until we were gods, and
then we played cornhole outside in the yard;
(to have gone bowling would have been a penance.)

There was no rule saying I couldn't wander away from
the group. There was no reason I should push the line
any further than reason; there was no immediate reason.

I am peering through the fence and seeing the sky
for the first time. Will we meet again; and what am I
doing? I'm asking—you're asking.

I'm wondering. The past is so boring, I'm wanting to let
it go. I kicked over a bucket but then bowled the planets
into the sun pin of gold.

Just pulse out the pain and circulate the misery. Just fall
in love and give into forgetting. Damn near to end, believe
compassionately; give birth to stars orgasmically.

I love you, Mom, you taught me to eat—my feelings.
I love you so much—you suffered for me, but I lost
control of that black hole.

A friend's mom, drinking the dark matter of a constant
remembering. We recalled and impersonated an
almighty falsehood.

Dear dead Granddad, you are an ancient apology.
We decided to travel to the nearest star on a whim
but blew up in our own atmosphere.

Is any of this making sense? Josh says he was God
in a past life; (I found God dying in this life), and
fell out of love with the thought of a next life.

The Consequence

We are the consequence of food's imagination.
The lizards of men—eat men, and are no more
grateful for them than they are for termites, no
more concerned for their heritage than man is
for the roach.

They devour his eyes after his tongue, so that
they can taste him—tasting his own visions
in hallucinogenic pangs of hunger, unspeakable
now, that we begin to digest.

Cycles

Sometimes what has always seemed
to be a web of lies, apparently, becomes
a synchronous pattern of alternating
truth, which is only seen through
cooperating fluctuations of knowing.
Pure—incongruous, sweeping rain,
showers of exceptions to the rule,
brought to a calm, light drizzle.
Still, even with thundering overhead,
the steppes are cast with easy answers
by gods of perchance, negating wisdom,
collapsing into isolated preponderance.

Hermitage

These candles lit and weeping
are willing to believe anything,
and tilt their flaming heads
in confusion and excitement
at the slightest draft of wind.
A hermit is indignant and needs,
must slam the windows shut
and seal the door with blankets
stolen from his own floor pallet.
He beckons himself to be still,
for fear of an irrational thought
of wild, flailing appendages not
reserved enough for quietude.
He returns for study with caution,
as he's discovered an assailing
nature, which is disconcerting.

Something We Lost

We feel like we've lost something,
and it's like we're dying to get it
back—whatever it is that we've lost.
And I think we'd have to die to get it
back, but only for a little while; and
then we'd have to chase after it for a
time before we remember, we have
to die to get it back.

Stave

Five weeks to the day left of summer
and maybe it should be over soon, or
maybe the fall has left a leaf or two
cradled in suspended in-animation.
Boring as to crave as it were
—boredom in the grave.

End of Shift

All of time exists at once in flux,
and if you gaze on a distance of cities
from on top a tower from the west,
you might, if your eyes are sober,
see the eastern ruins of former being,
as it may reflect a century at minimum.
The most you could ever hope to witness
—the least you could ever want to be.

Blacklight

We're all just dead and denim, dusty hair—up
here and down there. We look like moon ghosts
dancing in ancient photography; our skin burns
of flammable decency.

No more bad breath or blemishes, all our love
could not save us from our fetishes. So many
one-dimensional triangles leaning on each other
could not build a pyramid.

Yea, and we're all so dead and denim, dried-up
flair from some old nightmare. We act like cartoon
goats for talk show hosts, antsy with filmography
—our thin ferns of affable delinquency.

No more radical death or scrimmages, all our love,
and such brave red kisses. One intentional lie tangles
meaning up with some other. We ought to all be so
mired in the Id, and we're also dead and denim.

Sword Etiquette

These three things are separate forms
of each other: the faithful; the honest;
and the integral.

There are two other things and then all else: the door;
and the sword. The sword happens to be all three forms,
as the door is the consequence of any one form by itself
and will not open.

The body is a temple that wants to topple—over or under,
because really, it doesn't matter. Any way it falls, at once
or many times of a course, through that incessant coming
down, collapsing in on the ghosts of its constructors—
each year, a decade.

Each year, seeming like centuries. And the days and the nights
are archetypes of the mind, which never found a way around it-
self; except through the door, that only leads back inside,
where all things are separate, save for the sword—but
the sword does not abide the empty, nor does it doubt
the impermanence of mortals.

Moneyed Monkeys
and Holy Whores

Aggressively eating the progressively cheating,
an incessantly drinking and decadent faun.
Abusively beering and compulsively weeping,
heroically beating my progressive
hu-manatee[SIC] dumb.

As of something pertaining to the latently lacking
in the colors of Oden singing a pedestrian song,
for as empting melee and blooming here in May,
the pruning matinee has begun grooming—
blooming passionately all day.

Affinity leering through the sustaining earwig,
deaf and collapsing under such tone and laughing.
Something, something, something—something.
Humanity relapsing for the umpteenth time,
Harassing our own illnesses.

Faux Pas

Your world I felt denied,
your word—I would have lied.
And on it goes.

Of course, the wound got old.
A course—oh, quivering—hold.
Yeah, there it goes.

These seams are sewn 'long-side,
those dreams we all must hide.
So, no one knows,

what else or what's not told,
or else we be so bold.
And on it goes.

The Moth That Went Out of My Mind

I began my bedtime ritual
of touring the house, turning
lights off and on rapidly in
numerological patterns.

I noticed a moth flying against
the French door windowpanes
that lead onto the backyard patio,
as though they would eventually
give into a brutal persistence.

I felt responsible for attracting its
primitive impulses with my own. So
I cut off the light one final time and left
the poor brute to forget its passions, and
stay outside as I traveled to bed in a re-
current dream of flickering fluorescent light.

Cancer

You were thinking about her as you drove, a highway
dark and very old. You almost hit a coyote. You're not

dreaming; you woke up late for work—a little while ago.
Strung out from dreaming some angel knows the way to

Heaven, but you still can't remember the miles thus far,
between here and home. Whatever may come, the other

side is often blinding. You feel what fear should have been
but only because you felt it—when? Remember then,

the days were sometimes beautiful. And in that moment
you said a prayer, in an instant without a care.

(Alright God, I'm ready, so let's hear some music.)
Your foot gets heavy as the stations turn; static soothes

what cannot yearn. When pain is second nature, hope is
nothing. The world is dead, yet somehow, lives to die again,

and you continue as always—past and leaving,
but turn your lights off—and leave your lights off.

Mom is Dying

You God—you let me cry why forever. You could
kill a cow while geese fly north for summer. No
rain, but a cloud passes by for supper.

You cry, you beg—I submit to order.
I'll beg too—money, drugs, alcohol,
pussy, love, please!

In the beginning, so too in the end—I'm leaving.
Mom is dying so too could she have peace?
And in the next life, I will make music,

not just merely poetry.
And in the next life, I will make love,
not just lust for ecstasy.

And in the next life, I'll be sober, not
drunk but lovely, alive, though getting older.
And in the next life, we'll grow old—forever.

Mom

They don't know what eyes are for,
that's why they're only listening.
They can't see a shadow pass—
by a collapsing and exploding star.

Always and from now on, I'll gaze
on space from wherever you are
and want forever to be there with you,
as you were—not as you are.

As I've seen happen to you from beside
your hospice bed, where I look on,
and pray to heaven that it knows
just where to find you.

And suppose I never gave a damn, I'd still
love you from the time I woke up from hell
—reincarnated into your forgiving arms.

As I've felt with mine and being aware of
—an inconceivable time. You'll not be here
with us, as we say our goodbyes.

How could a word pass through this dying
place and still not find you? How could a name
so sacred as the Lords not resurrect you?

Andromeda will collide with our galaxy before
I forget about you. All the stars in heaven can't
shine on me without being reminded of you.

In the end, I'll look for only the most beautiful
—loveliest gloom. I'll call out to you in the dark,
in fear of our doom.

Hospice

I posit, the reason we build roofs on our houses
is not to shield us from the rain but to blind us

to the stars. Sardonic impressions ask an identity
to relent but they just don't know anymore.

A deathbed congregation of souls in denial of the flesh
as they defile tranquil minds with idiomatic prayers.

These beautiful fools are too old not to see through glamor.
I was thinking about this as I drove, and it seemed that a

light was green but it was red with no yellow in between,
so I had to stop suddenly. And how long I was stopped

once it turned—I couldn't tell you. But I can tell you, no
amount of road noise can make you forget the sound

of your mother groaning under her dying memories.
You see, I'm on my way somewhere that dies slowly

and painfully. And now that I'm here again—
I'm here again. Why is she still here?

Dying Light

Cancer allows time to become used to the idea
of having someone you love taken away
in pieces from their insides out—it doesn't

carry you or those you love away on a cloud,
or explode your being with awesome revelations
and light shows; it slowly stalks and at last pounces,

in a cosmic motion too ancient to detect. It is a predator
as old as time and exists. It exists, surely as we do,
and is as slow to its own conclusion as we are

to our own acceptance—that our time is of a finitude
more burdensome than sunsets, more worrisome
than the uncertainty of dawn.

A Dead Mother's Love

We're not even dealing with it; we're watching her die
as if she had died centuries ago. We probably shouldn't
smoke or drink anymore. We all just have to work
tomorrow; and I'm just running through this world—a
Dilaudid drip and a respirator.

What would—can worry me like nobody else. I want
to scream, but profanity. I whisper internally, my spirit's
flesh shell—eternity. I've been to Hell damn it! Why can't
I accept Heaven? Why, or why else?

My words are wearing gloves and you are wielding swords.
The moon is my shield; the stars are my armor, every
constellation is a chain link.

The earth is your horse and you are still beating her. She will
betray you, but by God, have I forgiven her. She deserves
every bit of it, and so won't we all?

Upon Waking We Die

Because fate is not a passion, she won't show her skin.
she won't, I've tried her—she is not a person.
No longer is my mother; insists she knows me,
and I've known her—all my life.
Her ashes hiding, somewhere I can't look,
over there, somewhere. Her faith no more—confiding.
No more abiding her torment, nor mine.
Under duress, undressed—dancing diamonds dying.
Crying, searching peace, for peace.
Please—please.
Death's aroma minding—reminding me,
undressing me of lies, preparing me to die.
So it only tastes like this, dusty, lustrous loving—oh, for all
about a while. We were both children, born from a goodnight kiss.

Our Motherless Remains

More of her in the drains
than her cremains, what remains
of our remains. We are the remains
of what remains of her, in this house
—is in the drains.
Not her cremated remains, but her
remnant hair and skin, and all those
remains. All that remains of her as
we remain, all that remains of us
—is in the drains.

The Universe I'll Love for You

I'd reach for you, though I don't know what spatial
dimension now holds to you. My hand is compelled
by chemical, electrical impulses in a mind that never
let go of you. In my dreams, memories play like reruns
with alternate endings and portrayals of you; my brain
retreats from the zenith—that my eyes convey
in distorted conceptions of what has become and what
still remains of you—in a world that is bereft of you.

The nadir becomes that horizon, which goes far around,
always to the same point that is farthest from the sight
of you. The sky goes only so high before an atmosphere
that protects us from an infinite that is only reminiscent
of you, then becomes a barrier that keeps us from reaching
out but not from looking up at you. This leaves us praying
with numb hands upon this beaten earth with naught but
tears to wash from us—what was you, but now is yet
the ashen late of you.

And the stars are merely silver—gray that must become
of dust—what beautiful rising embers that will always
wait for you, in a cold but beautiful universe that continues
to somehow expand, pulling us away from you, whether it
knows how much it hurts when we reach, yet cannot find
and so can only dream of you. And such a pleasant dream
could only mean an expanse, indeed, a depth so deep
with love that is always warm for you, and there for you.

Mom, I just want to tell you once more that I love you,
and that I will love this cold, dark universe, in spite of all
my anger, in spite of all my doubt. I must have faith that
even in death, if not for our Creator then for the mother
of our Creator—that I will love all of creation for you.
I will hate myself before I hate you; I will die before
I ever let go of you. I love you. And no matter what
may or may not be beyond, I will always love you.
RIP

Well, Then

Always in seclusion where it's safe to be sad;
passing by mirrors reminds me of my dad.
Living rooms are tombs and Mom is still dead,
no space left but memories on her side of the bed.
Their room is now just his room, and hers is in my head,
and inside my mind I'm already dead, recalling
every cruel word—that I ever said.

Seeing her faith abandon her in throes and gags,
reaching up out of still struggle—feeling rags.
Seeing in her eyes, shameful, desperate bags.
I project a telepathic consolation but it only nags.
She cries, she wants to go home—her spirit sags.
I suppress such a hatred for creation, that my
heart lags, still beating very slowly as life drags.

Forgive Ourselves

I can still hear you from the passenger seat
as you screamed out at me from behind
the wheel—that you would just crash
the car and kill us both; and I, screaming
back at you to go on and do it. I was a
petulant and passionate teenager, you were
my mother, mad as the world that made us.

Both mother and son dressed in cloth but naked
before the scrutiny of our fated, hated existence.
I still remember the way you told me the story
from the Bible, of the woman who touched Jesus'
garment and was healed by virtue of her faith,
the way you felt such a—connection to a woman
so ancient that her ailment must at last be cured
by death, long after such shame that she could
not bring herself to approach her savior but
merely to touch the robe that hung from the
stature of godliness.

But that was a child's perception of a woman who
he called Mom and the way she defined herself. I
thought you were afraid to look at yourself, but
while you were relating the gospels to me, I was
reading you, and I knew then just how aware you
were of yourself and how much you felt that you
needed to be saved; but I wouldn't know until just
now, the irony that your cancer started as cervical.

That you must have felt unclean as the woman
in the crowd that had believed she would be saved
if only she could reach out and touch the cloth
of such holiness—that would forgive her. I still
remember the rest of the car ride home, not just
the stretch where we hated each other.

I think about how good you often were to me even
when I was undeserving of forgiveness; how you gave
me the coat you were wearing at your brother's funeral
when I interrupted your grievous tears to tell you that I
was cold, but then you hurried away in search of your
mother. And I realized then that mothers are saviors, as I
realize now my own shame at having kept you on a cross
for so long, that I too have wept.

I remember our long talks and the long walks we sometimes
took together before you got sick and took to bed; the way
you did sometimes even before that. I often think of you
on my own walks, solitary now; and when I take to bed
myself, I pray that my faith be restored so that I see you
again, beyond life and death and both our depression.
That, maybe, if we remove our tattered garments,
we might be cured of our angry, sad and lonely selves
and that, maybe, to forgive each other
would be to—forgive ourselves.

There is That

I've lived other lives before;
I can feel them,
though I can't remember,
(each one—an impression.)
I have to realize,
when bright rage looms up
that now is to recall,
and when a dark age turns up,
that now is not all
that there is.

Nap

Death is coming down,
no point being sad.
Life is going 'round,
forgetting what is said.
Death is coming down;
nobody feels this bad.
Life just makes a sound,
hides beneath a bed.

Judith Shepherd

As you fell, so you lie
in wait,
to be found by anyone
but I found you,
(in your revelatory pose)
it seemed like.
You were so cold and when
I touched you,
uncertainty fell itself upon me.
Your silk nighty strewn across
the floor—as though,
it were still sliding off you.
Your nakedness so stunning,
I shivered.
A search, I felt for a pulse
but found no life.
I looked out your window
and saw only what is there
not what was.
(What was there—
but not what had been.)

For AJ. Farewell

Landmarks route the way back home;
classic mistakes repeat themselves.
Memories lose their way sometimes,
like comatose sleep must seem,
when eyes remember the lake
and how it has always felt
in August. Limbic brains must ride
waves of blue 'cross rippled skies,
to chance the wake of mother goose.
Her V formations coincide with heaven
and earth so fair whenever at sea,
yet never too far from familiar shores.

Constant Rebirth

The dead are without identity;
they are unquestioning servants.
Of course, we are afraid to be
still with them, alone with them.
Alive as we are born unwilling
to remain one with them.

Conversations with the Enlightened One

You should not be wondering so far in time,
he said. Is this very far? He nods and smirks.
So why are you here? I ask.
Me? He says—oh, I've always been here.
So have I? Umm, he considers the question.
Not yet, he meditates. I say, but I've never
been here before. He bows and snickers,
and then answers, but you will someday.
Is that someday now? I don't know,
he's saying. Was it?

Let This Pass

I died a thousand years ago;
I died a thousand times before now.
I'm only going home after a long day out;
I'm only going home, and I've been there
a thousand times before now,
a thousand times—only how?
Like when at an hourly paying job,
I'm just running out the clock
until it's time to finally go home.
Only, I don't know where home is.
There's no hope, so I contend with air;
there's no hope, so I intend not to dream.

Photograph

Still casting shadows,
still shedding skin.
Wade out of shallows,
no longer then.
Waving grave hallos,
so, how have you been?

Come and be Embraced

I'm always changing;
it's so hard to stay the same.
Identities seem so presumptuous,
presuming to be important,
or to matter at all.
My gifts are of a plentiful variety,
of which my most cherished of all
is always giving itself away
to the strangers that I become,
from one to another in passing
—moments are reincarnating.
Impermanence and happenstance
are dancing with me between them.
Their footwork is seldom staggering,
yet I am swept from mine.
And like a doll I am held and carried,
not tossed about—but kissed and married.
But if they were to let go of one another,
it would be alright that I fall.

Ripples in the Water

There's no room to move around freely.
My chest is tight so I can't breathe;
I feel like I'm drowning in the presence
of anxiety, dating back to a long past.
Music stirs the depths of hypersensitivity;
TV enables surface-level self-inflections.
I am the preyed-upon remains of life, a
corpse deposited into a retention by killers.
I can only wait here; if I thrash I will plunge
to the very bottom where there is no light.
If I cry, there is no noticeable difference.
I am what's left of the preconceptions
of a lost civilization, the dormant springtime
of a dying world, soon to wake up and realize.
I need to be calm in nature; I want to sleep in
the universe like the dead in the soil. I have to
be calm and not scare away mortality and the
peace of sleep in death. I must be still;
I must not will.

Magnitudes

I wouldn't be able to accurately explain
—but even if I could, you wouldn't understand,
and even if you did, you wouldn't even care—
but since you ask, or even if you never did,
as people often feel so obligated to do,
just for the sake of making conversation,
for silence to humans is like that
of the grave.

But if you can't glean an answer from my glance,
then there isn't time enough, as I am just ahead
of you all, and I can see what we are being
pushed fatefully near.

You will find out yourself soon enough, as I have
come close enough to marvel at the ledge
of my own consciousness, and having seen
glimpses of another side, have felt the soft
and loose ground below, give way to the steep,
uneven falling away of souls into a deep, dark
—quantum drain, where the space of our minds
become sealed away from time and sound, as light
can never enter, but exist only to turn your attention
to sights less hopeless or awful.

The Sky

We're not this guy; we came to die,
the world was damned before us.
We needn't cry, these things and I,
but, of course, we'll form a chorus.
Let out a sigh, from too deep inside,
this life that has died before us.
Not even a crime, but destiny lied,
still not a fate too terrible for us.
Too late this time, something inside
has chosen not to adore us.
The man is tied to his pitiful pride,
and wants only to be like Horus.

Life Is Death that Once Was Living

Destiny tells a joke;
fate is no friend of mine.
The faithless rip apart
—the fearful die again.
Sex is from earth;
love is from outer space.
Betrayal does not exist,
and real is not relevant.
Alone is by itself, but
sleep means everything.
Life is for the dead
—I am tired.
Sadness leaves you alone,
it's the only feeling that doesn't.
The food smells like corpses;
a drink can't offer condolences.
(Not in this life,)
that's the feeling I get.
No one understands
anything that matters.

Some Awful Thing Inside of Me

I know what you are so make no mistake, your amygdala being suffers me—and I suffer you, for all your memories; and I too remember—you are but a fate and I've named you; you're so much like hate that I've blamed you.

You are the one with the knife, sleepwalking through murderous visions, making small incisions in this conscious, sentient life that I must endure, with or without the grace of identity.

I have still not yet become you, in all your better lives—I cannot betray you. I pretend not for what—that which lives or dies, and I'll no longer feed you, the meat that you're so thirsty for, and you will not devour me—that part of you that you don't want to see, but here we are together in this existential sea.

So, look around. Decide what else you'd rather be, and see—all that worldly diversity, and stay with me, and be alone inside of me; become a very small part of me, and lie there very still beside me, until we're more like me, until we're far more likely.

No Connection

Universes loosely bond together for a while, sticky, surface-level connectors, never penetrating their respective, neighboring orbits, like foamy bubbles forming together on the surface of water— polluted with desperation for touch, and become perverted with the need for attention.

Isolation extends so far as the most lost, but does not ever come back to a whole; nor was there ever a whole from the start.

And the beginning was indistinguishable from the end, as the in-between was comparable to nothing.

So now, here we all are, sharing the experience of being alone —each of us.

A Friend in Need

Envy? Do you really want to be angry, lonely,
isolated from the rest of humanity?

Empty—feeling for you as me, crying dryly
from some depleted source of vanity.

Hollow—voices calling to me but through echo,
telling me nothing of themselves,

or of you, asking me nothing revealing.
Hello, noises cawing in me but through echo,

yelling something at my selves, or to you,
basking in something I'm feeling.

Alone, masking sadness with a common tone,
tasking madness with the unknown.

Atone, asking of sadness all that I've known,
begging of madness all on my own.

Drive Thru

I thought I saw the future; that was insane.
I could imagine an end that was humane.
I heard the word cancer in the profane.
I felt poorly in a vision of all of our pain.
I thought it was a lesson—it was the rain;
I was always alone down by the drain.
A feeling other than that I could feign.
Another sign or omen, therein a stain.
A ceiling soiled softly as the mundane,
another perfect life lived all in vain.

Living Dead All Along

Opened a door; what for—what for?
A thousand deaths; what more—what more?
Deep in a breath, one final more; a gust of wind,
a sigh—a war.

Offend some more; a bore—a bore.
A thousand deaths, but more—oh, more.
Sleep in-depth, one final more; a gust
of wind, a lie—assure.

Often one more; a chore—a chore.
A thousand breaths—yet more, and more.
Steep is the breadth, one offal for; a lust
of wind—to die, to bore.

Time is a Nazi

Cruelty—you will see,
the world will turn and then you'll see.
As the sky is blue and so the sea,
the world will turn to darkened glee.
Cruelty—you will see,
the world will turn and then you'll see.
As what once was, will come to be,
(as with Zyklon B and World War Three)
the world will turn on you and me.

Vegan Friendly

Is that why we're here, to be treated like animals,
and to treat others like animals, and to treat animals
the same way that we treat ourselves—like lifeless
morsels, incapable of kindness?

Is that why we're all such animals? Is that why we hate
them so much, as to skin them alive and sell their fur
like it was ours to sell, like it was ours to take?

Are we all so ashamed to be gentle, that we have become
carnivorous? Have we only to prey upon ourselves to be
happy in our murderous fashions? Are we all so delectable
in our dead-skin suits that we'd rather consummate the dead
than to make love in an innocent way to one another?

What awful banquets we'll all be served—in Hell. What terrible
creatures will be fed with our quivering and lamented flesh?

I Just Want Out of Myself

Nature is speaking,
however much we do not listen.
I am listening now.
She is saying to us all,
although, I'm the one who is hearing,
"Come and be like us.
There, the moon—behind such clouds,
whose light is still.
Here, beside the stars,
all naked in the night,
whose dark you all are fearing.
We do not mind you at all,
yet in our late phase, you dream.
You can do without those bodies,
which are always dying.
You can be without the mind,
which is only ever seeming;
and a spirit that needs believing.
Come and be like us,
and never mind what else.
We will be together,
none of us are leaving."

Still Choosing Humility
Over Honor

Our existence in this life is evidence of nothing more
than having died to get here. Our mortality gifts to us
the one thing otherwise missing from the mundanity
of dying, and that is the blessing of tragedy, for without
it, as such would mean only comedy; and as feasible as
the notion, it is equally absurd to laugh for all of eternity.

It's like there's just not enough to go around.
Don't try talking to the sober while drunk;
you'll feel as though you've died and risen
in a holy land of dollar stores and thrift shops,
and imprisoned societies redeemed by money.
So, memorize the signs—of the times,
and the dialogues of playdough[Sic].

It's a quarter until four in the morning now, and I have to be
up early for work soon. But still, despite the temptation to give
up contemplation of mankind's quarrel—still, I'd prefer not to
give up drinking, like a success mounted atop a pile of failures,
or a better instinct all for its own destruction.

Existence and Imperfection

I've had the wind knocked right to hell out of my lungs
in a sudden flash of the past two decades and in waking
urgency. I have been flattened like a rug and trampled over,
while my head tries to bite for oxygen, and my mind
screams out in despair at having never been understood.
The planet just swarms about in all directions, save for
mine and fascination.

I am all but a dead actor and liquor cannot save me
from the next act as I'd believed it would save me
from the first or second. I'm only one—to perish
in a billion transparent miseries and fadeaway nothings.
I have seen a trillion stars shoot by like dreams
in an interdimensional spaceship, at the speed of light
between sleep and wakefulness, as my heart feigned beating.

That I have woken to the anxiety of my own labored breathing
is testament to existence, and much as well to imperfection.
The light of my being is dim and imperceptible except to those
clairvoyant. The time of a child has passed away, while a man
beats at his own chest in a drunken realization
of that child's mortality.

The life of a man is measured by a boy's liveliness in the midst
of these revelations. Both death and birth are intermediate
postures. The grave is a place between time, where the two
can reconcile an eternity wasted on addiction,
and loneliness—and despair.